P9-DEL-930

HEDGEHOGS

by Josh Gregory

Children's Press®

An Imprint of Scholastic Inc.

Content Consultant
Dr. Stephen S. Ditchkoff
Professor of Wildlife Sciences
Auburn University
Auburn, Alabama

Photographs ©: Folkert Christoffers/age fotostock; 1: Eastmanphoto/
Dreamstime; 2 background, 3 background: Karlien Du plessis/
Dreamstime; 2 main: G Pohl/age fotostock; 3 main: G Pohl/age
fotostock; 4, 5 background: Eyal Bartov/Alamy Images; 5 top inset:
Juniors Bildarchiv GmbH/Alamy Images; 5 bottom inset: F Hecker/age
fotostock; 6, 7: Stephen Dalton/Science Source; 8, 9: Minden Pictures/
Superstock, Inc.; 10, 11: age fotostock/Superstock, Inc.; 12, 13: G
Pohl/age fotostock; 14, 15: Les Stocker/Alamy Images; 16, 17: Gerard
Lacz Images/Superstock, Inc.; 18, 19: Biosphoto/Superstock, Inc.; 20,
21: Arco/C & R Doerr/age fotostock; 22, 23: Biosphoto/Superstock,
Inc.; 24, 25: NHPA/Superstock, Inc.; 26, 27: Isselee/Dreamstime; 28:
Juniors Bildarchiv GmbH/Alamy Images; 31: Illustration by Michael
Long. © The Natural History Museum/The Image Works; 32, 33: Eyal
Bartov/Alamy Images; 34, 35: Nicholas Smythe/Science Source; 36,
37: Nature Picture Library/Alamy Images; 38, 39: Wildlife GmbH/
Alamy Images; 40, 41: F Hecker/age fotostock; 44, 45 background:
Karlien Du plessis/Dreamstime; 46: Eastmanphoto/Dreamstime.

Library of Congress Cataloging-in-Publication Data
Gregory, Josh, author.
  Hedgehogs / by Josh Gregory.
    pages cm. — (Nature's children)
  Summary: "This book details the life and habits of hedgehogs"—
Provided by publisher.
  Includes bibliographical references and index.
  ISBN 978-0-531-21390-2 (library binding : alk. paper) —
ISBN 978-0-531-21493-0 (pbk. : alk. paper)
  1. Hedgehogs—Juvenile literature. I. Title. II. Series: Nature's children
(New York, N.Y.)
  QL737.E753G74 2016
  599.33'2—dc23   2014043978

Printed in China 62
SCHOLASTIC, CHILDREN'S PRESS, and associated logos are
trademarks and/or registered trademarks of Scholastic Inc.

1 2 3 4 5 6 7 8 9 10 R 25 24 23 22 21 20 19 18 17 16

Hedgehogs

Class	Mammalia
Order	Erinaceomorpha
Family	Erinaceidae
Genera	5 genera
Species	16 species
World distribution	Africa, Europe, Asia, New Zealand
Habitats	Grasslands, fields, deserts, forests
Distinctive physical characteristics	Entire body, except for face, ears, legs, and underside, is covered in pointed spines; fur and spines are various shades of white, black, and brown; short legs; long claws on feet; pointed face with relatively large eyes
Habits	Mostly nocturnal; lives a solitary lifestyle during most of the year; rolls up into a ball and uses pointy spines to defend itself from predators; makes piglike snorting sounds as it searches for food; relies mainly on senses of smell and hearing
Diet	Carnivorous; mostly eats small invertebrates such as insects, spiders, and worms; sometimes eats animals such as mice, snakes, lizards, and frogs; sometimes eats fruit or eggs

Contents

CHAPTER 1

Prickly Protection

Along the edge of a peaceful field in the English countryside, near a stand of trees, a red fox waits motionless. The fox is on the lookout for a meal. It watches carefully for signs of movement in the grassy field. Eventually, it spots a small hedgehog nosing around for prey of its own. At first, the hedgehog does not notice the nearby threat. But just as the fox crouches down and prepares to attack, the hedgehog catches its scent on the breeze. The hedgehog immediately springs into action by rolling up into a tight ball. The prickly spines covering its body point straight out in every direction. The fox snaps at the hedgehog, then backs away as it realizes that its attacks are of little use. Instead of continuing the fight, it runs off in search of easier prey. Once the coast is clear, the hedgehog unrolls itself and goes back to its business. Thanks to its handy defenses, it will live to see another day.

It is hard for most predators to get past a hedgehog's prickly spines.

Small and Spiny

There are many different hedgehog species around the world. Though each one has features that set it apart, they all share a very similar physical appearance. Hedgehogs have short, stumpy bodies. Their legs and tails are also quite stubby. At the end of each foot are several toes with long, sharp claws.

A hedgehog's spines are its most distinctive feature. These pointy structures cover the animal's entire body except for its face, ears, legs, and underside. These spineless parts of the body are covered in fur. Both the fur and spines are shades of white, black, and brown.

Hedgehogs are not very large animals. Most of them weigh less than 1.5 pounds (0.7 kilograms). Even the largest species, the west European hedgehog, reaches a maximum weight of around 2.4 pounds (1.1 kg). A fully grown hedgehog measures between 5.5 and 12 inches (14 and 30.5 centimeters) from the tip of its nose to the base of its tail. The tail measures an additional 0.4 to 2.4 inches (1 to 6 cm).

Adult male
6 ft. (1.8 m)

European hedgehog
12 in. (30.5 cm) long

Hedgehogs that live in deserts, such as the long-eared hedgehog, usually have longer ears and legs than other types of hedgehogs.

Hedgehog Homes

Hedgehogs are found in many different parts of the world. Some species are native to sections of Africa. One species lives throughout the central portion of the continent, while another occupies the south. There is also a species found only in the country of Somalia. Other species range across much of Europe, with one species found mainly in the west and another in the east. There are also hedgehogs native to parts of Asia.

Because various hedgehog species live in such a wide range of locations, their habitats often vary greatly. Some hedgehogs live in forests, while others are found in fields or grasslands. Many live in desert areas. Some live in areas that experience cold, icy winters, while others deal with hot, dry weather all year long. As a result, different hedgehog species can have very different lifestyles.

The north African hedgehog has spread from Africa's northern areas to parts of Europe and certain African islands.

CHAPTER 2

Built for Success

Hedgehogs have many abilities and physical features that help them survive in the wild. Like all animals, they rely on a range of senses to help them communicate, find food, navigate, and avoid danger. Because hedgehogs have large, round eyes, it might seem natural to assume that vision is one of their most important senses. However, hedgehogs actually have poor eyesight. In addition, they are most active at night, when there is little light by which to see. As a result, a hedgehog's senses of hearing and smell are far more important.

The wide, curved shape of a hedgehog's ears enables it to collect sounds from all around. Some species have especially long ears, giving them even better hearing.

A hedgehog's sense of smell is also very strong. This animal has a special feature called a Jacobson's organ inside its nasal passages. The Jacobson's organ allows a hedgehog to "taste" odors in the air. This helps it detect scents that could not be smelled otherwise.

A long-eared hedgehog uses its big ears to listen for potential prey and enemies.

On the Move

For the most part, hedgehogs live close to the ground. They usually move around their environments by walking carefully, with their body kept low. This is not a very fast way to get around. However, hedgehogs can pick up the pace when they really need to. They do this by extending their legs and rising up to their full height. This pushes their body up off the ground and gives them room to take longer strides. Running this way takes a lot of energy, though, so a hedgehog can speed along for only a short time before getting tired.

Some hedgehog species need to deal with obstacles such as trees, rocks, and bodies of water. Luckily, they are well equipped for such situations. Many hedgehogs are good climbers. Their sharp claws allow them to grip a variety of surfaces. Hedgehogs can also swim, using their paws as paddles.

FUN FACT! Hedgehogs are named for the piglike snorting and grunting sounds they make as they sniff out prey.

A west European hedgehog makes its way steadily across a pond.

A Diverse Diet

As a hedgehog shuffles along through its habitat, it keeps its nose low to the ground and sniffs constantly. It also pauses from time to time to lift its head and sniff the air above. As it sniffs, it hopes to catch a whiff of potential prey. Hedgehogs sniff out most of their prey under plants, in grass, or just below the surface of the soil. They stick their pointy faces into these hiding spots and use their sharp teeth to bite and kill the prey.

A hedgehog's diet is made up mainly of other animals. Hedgehogs usually hunt for insects and other small invertebrates. They sometimes eat larger animals, too. Though diet varies based on species and location, most hedgehogs enjoy prey such as worms, slugs, and snails. Lizards, mice, and frogs are also on the menu for some species. Hedgehogs even eat poisonous animals such as spiders, scorpions, and snakes. In addition, they sometimes eat eggs, mushrooms, and fruit.

Two hedgehogs share an earthworm.

Staying Safe

Though hedgehogs are skilled hunters, they are also preyed upon by a number of powerful predators. Depending on where they live, hedgehogs might have to defend against such enemies as badgers, foxes, and dogs. Other hedgehogs face off against big snakes or deadly birds of prey such as owls or hawks.

Hedgehogs are not likely to outrun most of these predators. Instead, they hold their ground and rely on their pointy spikes for protection. When a hedgehog is in danger, it curls its body into a ball, tucking its head and legs underneath itself. Its spines all point straight outward, forming a shield that is tough for most animals to break through. However, a hedgehog is not completely safe when it is rolled up. Some predators poke their muzzles into the soft area where the hedgehog folds its body. Birds simply use their long claws and tough feet to reach through the spines. If a hedgehog survives this attack, a bird might lift it into the air and drop it on the ground to injure it.

A hedgehog's predators are usually much larger than it is.

Hot and Cold

Many hedgehogs live in areas where they must deal with extreme weather. These species all have skills and behaviors that allow them to thrive in climates where other animals would not survive. Hedgehogs that live in habitats with icy winters hibernate during the coldest parts of the year. During hibernation, hedgehogs crawl into a safe burrow and go into a deep sleep that lasts for weeks. During this time, they do not use as much energy as they do while awake, so they don't need as much food. In the weeks and months before winter, they eat a lot of food to help build up fat. The extra fat keeps them warm and provides a source of energy through the long, cold months.

Hedgehogs living in areas with very hot, dry summers use a technique similar to hibernation to help them beat the heat and avoid getting too thirsty. It is called estivation. The hedgehogs crawl underground or underneath plants to stay out of the sun. Then they go into a deep sleep.

Hedgehogs build a warm nest of leaves and grass when it is time to hibernate.

CHAPTER 3

Living and Growing

Throughout most of the year, a hedgehog typically leads a solitary lifestyle. It rarely interacts with other hedgehogs. However, hedgehogs are not territorial. When they do happen to meet one another, they do not fight.

During the day, hedgehogs stay hidden away in nests or burrows. There, they sleep while rolled into a ball for protection against surprise attacks in case predators discover them. Some hedgehogs build nests out of leaves, twigs, and other plant parts. Others dig holes in the ground to form burrows, or they use burrows that have been abandoned by other animals. A series of hedgehogs might use the same nest or burrow. However, they never use the same one at the same time.

After waking up in the evening, hedgehogs leave their resting places and begin searching for food. They stay on the move as they hunt, and they can cover a distance of several miles over the course of a night.

A hedgehog peeks out of its burrow in France.

Meeting with Mates

The only time adult hedgehogs actively seek out one another is when it comes time for them to **mate**. The timing of a hedgehog's mating season varies widely from species to species. For example, the season lasts from roughly October to March for the north African hedgehog, but stretches from April to September for the west European hedgehog.

During mating season, male hedgehogs seek out females that are ready to produce young. The females release special scents when it is time for them to mate. A male notices these scents and approaches the female, who then decides whether or not she wants to mate with him.

After mating, the male does not stay to assist his mate or care for his young. Instead, he heads off to begin looking for another mate. A male hedgehog tries to reproduce with as many females as he can during mating season.

A male west European hedgehog approaches a female during mating season in southern England.

Hedgehog Parenting

A mother hedgehog gives birth to a litter of babies, called hoglets, around 30 to 50 days after mating. A litter might have anywhere from 1 to 11 hoglets. Depending on the species, the mother might mate again and give birth to a second or third litter during a single mating season.

Hedgehogs give birth inside burrows or nests, where it is easier to keep hoglets safe. Like other mammals, mother hedgehogs feed their babies by producing milk. Newborn hoglets are too small and weak to hunt for food on their own. They are born blind, and they lack the powerful spines of an adult. This means they cannot protect themselves by rolling into a ball yet. As a result, hoglets face many threats from predators. One of the biggest threats of all comes from other hedgehogs. Male hedgehogs see the young of their own species as potential food. Even mothers sometimes eat their own babies!

A hedgehog's first spines are not strong enough to keep it safe.

Going Through Changes

It does not take long for baby hedgehogs to become adults. Depending on the species, it takes anywhere from one to two months for a hoglet to grow up, leave its mother's nest, and begin an independent life. Some types of hedgehogs are born with a few soft, white spines, while others are born with no visible spines at all. But within the first few days of its life, a hoglet's stiff, pointy spines will begin to appear. During this time, the hedgehog's muscles also get stronger. Within a couple of weeks, the baby hedgehog will open its eyes for the first time. It will also become strong enough to roll into a ball. Soon after this, the hedgehog begins eating solid food and stops drinking its mother's milk.

After leaving its mother's nest for good, a young hedgehog wanders off to establish a **home range** of its own. By the time it is about one year old, it is ready to mate and have its own babies. If the hedgehog is lucky enough to avoid being eaten, it will likely live for around six to seven years in the wild.

The first time a baby explores the world outside the nest is often with its mother.

CHAPTER 4

The Family Tree

Hedgehogs are members of the family Erinaceidae. Erinaceids have existed on Earth for tens of millions of years. The first members of this family lived between 56 million and 34 million years ago. These early Erinaceids are the ancestors of the hedgehog species living today.

These early ancestors have been extinct for a very long time. Scientists have studied them and learned about the way they lived by unearthing fossils. One hedgehog ancestor that was discovered through fossils is *Deinogalerix*. Sometimes called the giant hedgehog, this animal lived around 10 million to 5 million years ago in the woods of western Europe. Like today's hedgehogs, it hunted for insects and other small animals. However, it did not have spines. This means it probably looked more like a rat than a hedgehog. Its body was around 2 feet (61 cm) long. That might not seem very big, but it is about twice as long as the largest of today's hedgehogs.

Deinogalerix *had a long snout and tail, and was covered in fur.*

Species to Species

Scientists classify today's hedgehogs into 5 **genera** and 16 species. The genus *Atelerix* consists of the four African hedgehog species. The four woodland species make up the *Erinaceus* genus. These species are the Amur hedgehog, the southern white-breasted hedgehog, the west European hedgehog, and the northern white-breasted hedgehog. The genus *Hemiechinus* includes the two long-eared hedgehog species. *Mesechinus* contains the Daurian hedgehog and the Hugh's hedgehog. Finally, the four desert hedgehogs are grouped together as *Paraechinus*.

The different hedgehog species all look a lot alike. However, there are small differences between each of them. For example, the west European hedgehog is larger than any of the others. The long-eared species, as their name implies, have ears that are noticeably larger than those of other hedgehogs. Other species have distinctive fur coloring. For example, the southern white-breasted hedgehog has a white patch on its chest. The Indian hedgehog is covered in white fur except for its black face and legs.

The southern white-breasted hedgehog is found across Turkey and as far south as Israel and Jordan.

Close Cousins

The hedgehog's closest living relative is the gymnure. Like hedgehogs, gymnures are members of the Erinaceidae family. As a result, they have a lot in common with each other. For example, they have similar body and face shapes. Gymnures are found in the forests of Southeast Asia. There, they lead a lifestyle that is much like a hedgehog's. They eat insects, worms, and other small animals. Some gymnure species are active only at night, but others also come out to search for food in the daylight.

The most obvious difference between gymnures and hedgehogs is that gymnures do not have spines. Instead, their bodies are covered in fur. As a result, they look a lot like rats. Because they lack spines, gymnures don't defend themselves by rolling into a ball the way hedgehogs do when threatened by enemies. Instead, gymnures fend off attackers by releasing a strong, unpleasant scent.

Gymnures and hedgehogs have common ancestors.

CHAPTER 5

Humans and Hedgehogs

Like all living things, hedgehogs play many important roles in maintaining the health of their habitats. They keep the populations of insects and other small animals from growing too large. They are also an important food source for many predators. Too few or too many hedgehogs in an area would affect the balance of the ecosystem.

A hedgehog's natural behaviors can be directly beneficial to humans. For example, many of the insects they eat are pests to people. As a result, they are a welcome sight in gardens, yards, and other areas populated by humans.

Unfortunately, contact with humans can have negative results for hedgehogs. Vehicles might hit hedgehogs that are trying to cross a busy road or street. Many hedgehogs also find their habitats shrinking as people expand towns and farms farther into the wilderness. In some places, hedgehogs are killed as a source of food.

A hedgehog can help a garden thrive.

Changing Populations

Overall, no hedgehog species is in danger of dying out anytime soon. However, these animals are slowly disappearing from specific areas. This is especially true in the United Kingdom, where the once-common west European hedgehog has become a rare sight. Scientists believe that this is because of habitat loss and the negative effects of changes in the climate.

On the other hand, some places have more hedgehogs than they can handle. Many years ago, humans brought hedgehogs to New Zealand and the islands of Scotland. They hoped the hedgehogs would kill pests in their gardens. However, hedgehogs do not live in these places naturally. As a result, they have few predators to keep their numbers in check. The hedgehogs eat large amounts of bird eggs and other local prey. This has caused some species' populations to shrink. To protect the native species, authorities in New Zealand and Scotland have been forced to begin killing the invasive hedgehogs.

In some parts of Europe, hedgehogs are struggling to survive alongside roads and human residences.

Pointy Pets

In addition to introducing hedgehogs to wild areas where they are not native, humans have brought these animals into their homes as pets. Hedgehogs can survive comfortably in captivity if they receive proper care. However, there are many drawbacks to keeping them as pets. Hedgehogs are often afraid of people even if their owners are very careful with them. In addition, they can carry a number of diseases and parasites that affect people and other pets.

Hedgehogs are much more than cute pets. They are wild animals that have an important place in the natural world. They deserve our respect. To ensure they continue to thrive far into the future, we must protect natural environments and avoid doing things that can harm wild animals and plants. For example, conservation groups in Great Britain are working to prevent local hedgehog populations from disappearing. Through efforts like these, we can make sure that hedgehogs have a place in our world for many years to come.

The west European hedgehog is one of the hedgehog species most commonly kept as a pet.

Words to Know

ancestors (AN-ses-turz) — ancient animal species that are related to modern species

burrow (BUR-oh) — a tunnel or hole in the ground made or used as a home by an animal

captivity (kap-TIV-i-tee) — the condition of being held or trapped by people

climates (KLYE-mitz) — the weather typical of places over long periods of time

conservation (kon-sur-VAY-shun) — the act of protecting an environment and the things that live in it

ecosystem (EE-koh-sis-tuhm) — all the living things in a place and their relation to the environment

extinct (ik-STINGKT) — no longer found alive

family (FAM-uh-lee) — a group of living things that are related to each other

fossils (FOSS-uhlz) — the hardened remains of prehistoric plants and animals

genera (JEN-ur-uh) — groups of related plants or animals that are larger than a species but smaller than a family

habitats (HAB-uh-tats) — places where an animal or a plant is usually found

hibernate (HYE-bur-nate) — to sleep through the winter in order to survive when temperatures are cold and food is hard to find

home range (HOME RAYNJ) — the area of land in which an animal usually spends most of its time

invasive (in-VAY-siv) — describing a plant or animal that is introduced to a new habitat and may cause that habitat harm invertebrates (in-VUR-tuh-brits) — animals without a backbone

litter (LIT-ur) — a number of baby animals that are born at the same time to the same mother

mammals (MAM-uhlz) — warm-blooded animals that have hair or fur and usually give birth to live young

mate (MAYT) — to join together to produce babies

muzzles (MUHZ-uhlz) — the noses or mouths of animals

native (NAY-tiv) — naturally belonging to a certain place

parasites (PAR-uh-sites) — animals or plants that live on or inside of another animal or plant

predators (PREH-duh-turz) — animals that live by hunting other animals for food

prey (PRAY) — an animal that's hunted by another animal for food

solitary (SOL-ih-tehr-ee) — preferring to live alone

species (SPEE-sheez) — one of the groups into which animals and plants of the same genus are divided

territorial (terr-uh-TOR-ee-uhl) — defensive of a certain area

Habitat Map

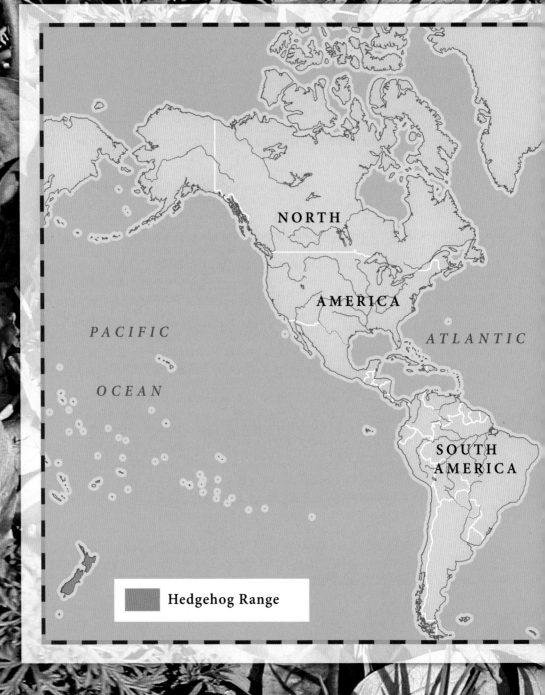

NORTH

AMERICA

PACIFIC

OCEAN

ATLANTIC

SOUTH
AMERICA

Hedgehog Range

ARCTIC OCEAN

EUROPE

ASIA

AFRICA

PACIFIC
OCEAN

INDIAN

OCEAN

OCEAN

AUSTRALIA

Find Out More

Books

Rockwood, Leigh. *Tell Me the Difference Between a Porcupine and a Hedgehog*. New York: PowerKids Press, 2013.

Schuetz, Kari. *Hedgehogs*. Minneapolis: Bellwether Media, 2013.

Visit this Scholastic Web site for more information on hedgehogs:
www.factsfornow.scholastic.com
Enter the keyword **Hedgehogs**

Index

Page numbers in *italics* indicate a photograph or map.

About the Author

Josh Gregory has written more than 80 books covering a wide range of subjects. He received a BA from the University of Missouri–Columbia. He works as a children's book editor and lives in Chicago, Illinois.